I0759743

# Feelings and Emotions

by E. Russell Primm III • illustrated by Kathleen Petelinsek

childsworld.com

**Published by The Child's World®**
800-599-READ • childsworld.com



**Photography Credits**
Sergey Novikov/Shutterstock.com, cover, 11; ESB Professional/Shutterstock.com, 1, 9; Ground Picture/Shutterstock.com, 3, 14, 20; Krakenimages.com/Shutterstock.com, 4; Anatta_Tan/Shutterstock.com, 5; Olena Yakobchuk/Shutterstock.com, 6; DenisProduction.com/Shutterstock.com, 7; Arsenii Palivoda/Shutterstock.com, 8; M-Production/Shutterstock.com, 10; Anna Kraynova/Shutterstock.com, 12; Sascha Burkard/Shutterstock.com, 13; Nicoleta Ionescu/Shutterstock.com, 15; Marlon Lopez MMG1 Design/Shutterstock.com, 16; DimaBerlin/Shutterstock.com, 17; Tyler Olson/Shutterstock.com, 18; leungchopan/Shutterstock.com, 19; fizkes/Shutterstock.com, 21

**ISBN Information**
9781503889019 (Reinforced Library Binding)
9781503890091 (Portable Document Format)
9781503891333 (Online Multi-user eBook)
9781503892576 (Electronic Publication)

**LCCN** 2023950370

**Printed in the United States of America**

**Note to Parents, Caregivers, and Educators:** The understanding of any language begins with the acquisition of vocabulary, whether the language is spoken or manual. The books in this series provide readers, both young and old, with basic American Sign Language signs. Combining close photo cues and simple, but detailed, line illustrations, children and adults alike can begin the process of learning American Sign Language.

Let these books be an introduction to the world of American Sign Language. Most languages have regional dialects and multiple ways of expressing the same thought. This is also true for sign language. We have attempted to use the most common version of the signs for the words in this series. As with any language, the best way to learn is to be taught in person by a frequent user. It is our hope that this series will pique your interest in sign language.

**A special thanks to our advisers:** As a member of a deaf family that spans four generations, **Kim Bianco Majeri** lives, works, and plays among the Deaf community. **Carmine L. Vozzolo** is an educator of children who are deaf and hard of hearing, as well as their families.

**E. Russell Primm III** was a well-known figure in the publishing industry who produced thousands of acclaimed books for children. He was affiliated with organizations such as the American Library Association, the Chicago Book Clinic, and the University of Chicago Publishing Program Advisory Board.

**Kathleen Petelinsek** has loved books since she was a child. Through the years, she has written, designed, and illustrated many books for children. She lives in Wisconsin, near her granddaughter who also shares her love for books.

Another word for amazed is "astonished."

# Amazed

Open and close your hands near your face. Repeat.

Another word for angry is "mad."

# Angry

Make claws with your hands. Start at your belly and pull outward and upward.

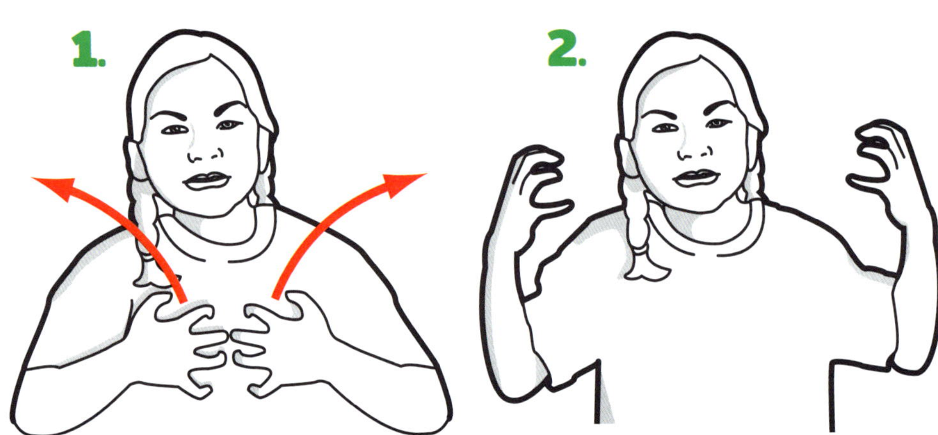

Another word for cranky is "grouchy."

# Cranky

Bend your fingers toward your face. Repeat.

Another word for disappointed is "downhearted."

# Disappointed

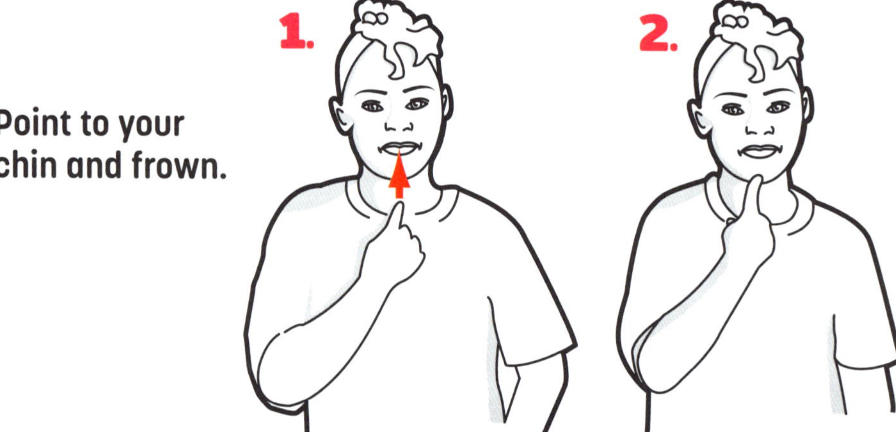


Point to your chin and frown.

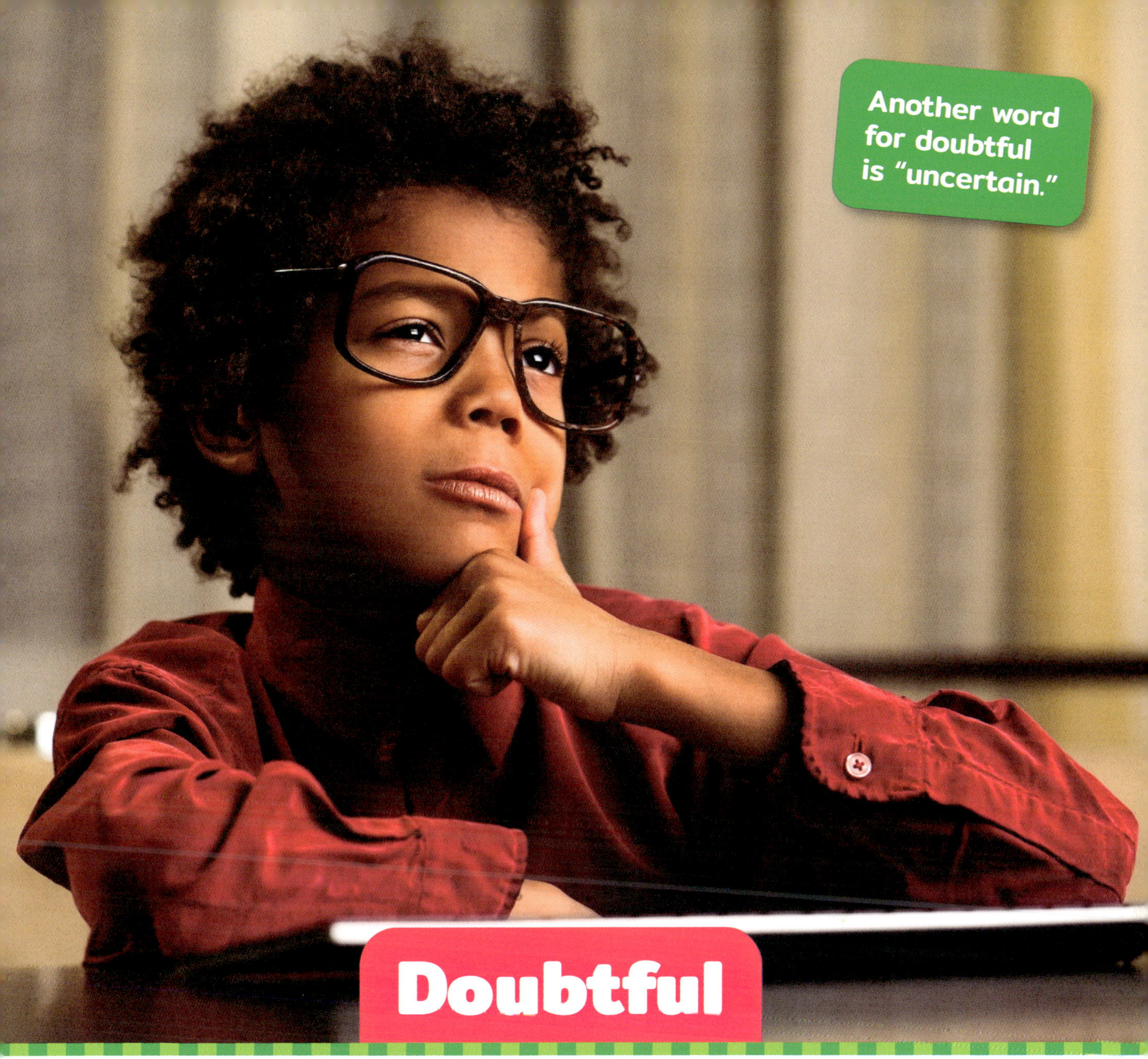

Another word for doubtful is "uncertain."

# Doubtful

Bend your fingers toward your face. Repeat.

Another word for frustrated is "irked."

# Frustrated

Smack the back of your hand (lightly) into your face twice.

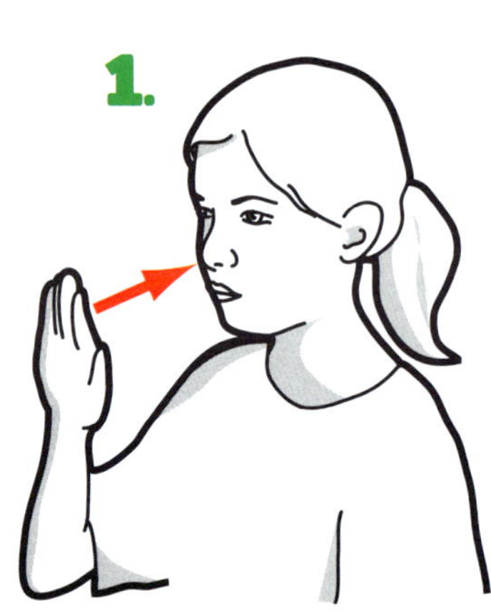

Another word for happy is "jolly."

# Happy

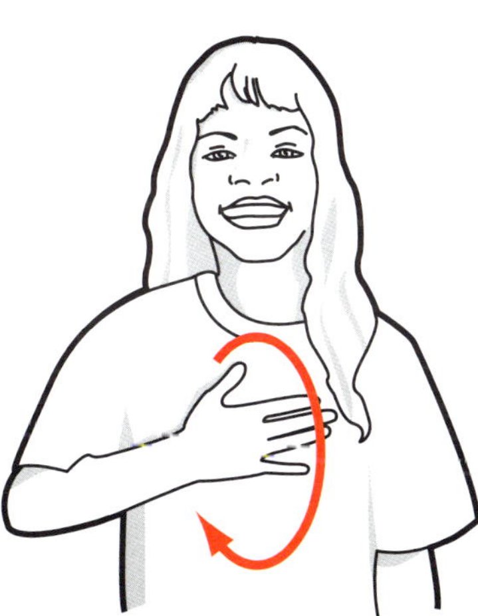

Place a flat hand on your chest. Quickly move up, out, and around in a loop (your palm always faces your chest). Repeat.

Another word for hurt is "wounded."

# Hurt

Point two fingers toward each other. Then twist in different directions (if your right hand twists clockwise, your left hand twists counterclockwise).

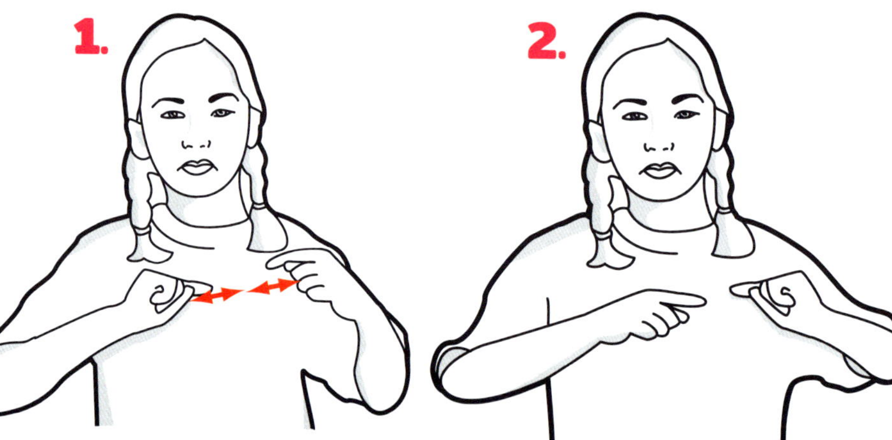

Another word for proud is "contented."

# Proud

Point your thumb at your belly. Move upward toward your chest.

Another word for puzzled is "confused."

# Puzzled

Point outward, then curl your finger and bring it to your forehead.

1.

2.

Another word for sad is "depressed."

# Sad

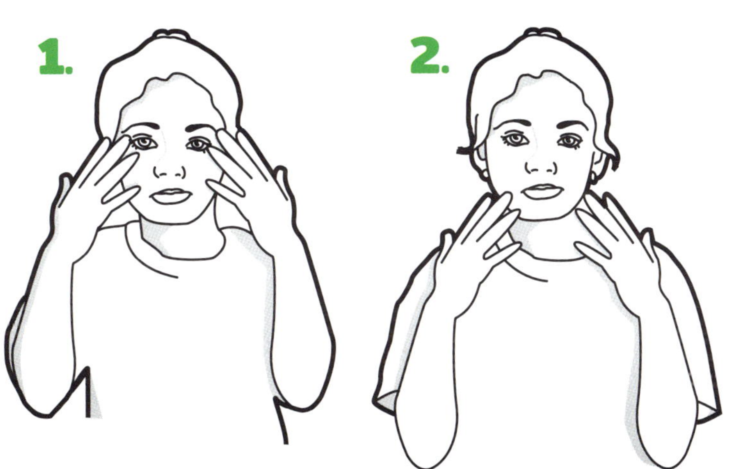


Make a sad face. Place both hands in front of your face and pull down, like tears.

Another word for satisfied is "appeased."

# Satisfied

Bring both flat hands in toward your chest at the same time.

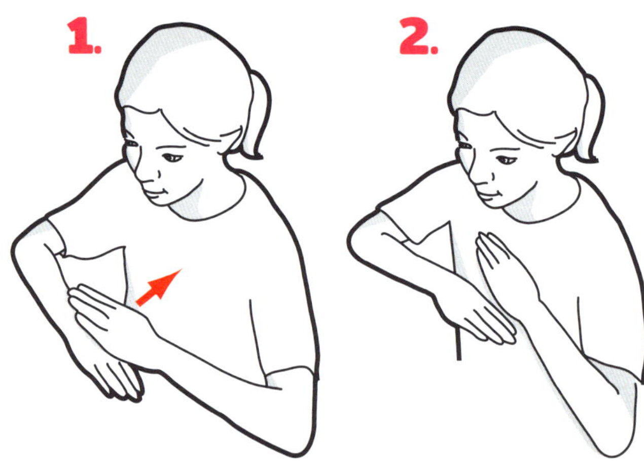

Another word for selfish is "greedy."

# Selfish

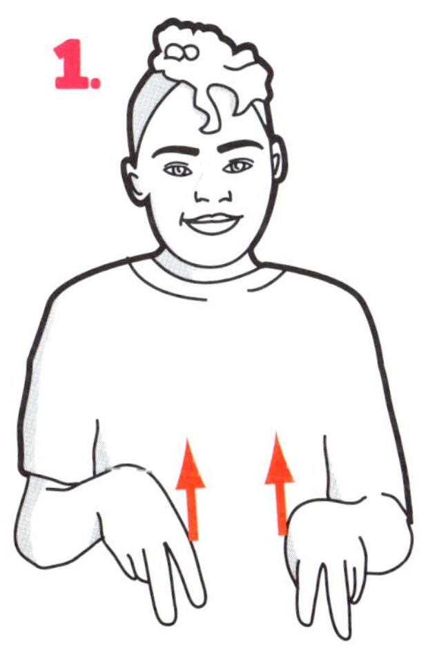

Pull your fingers in as if you are pulling something toward you.

Another word for shy is "bashful."

# Shy

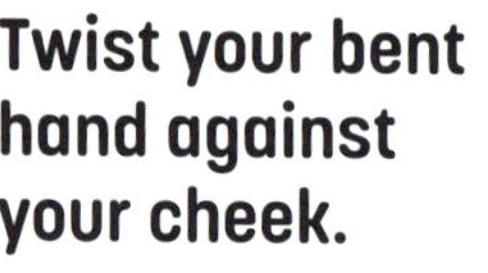

Twist your bent hand against your cheek.

1.

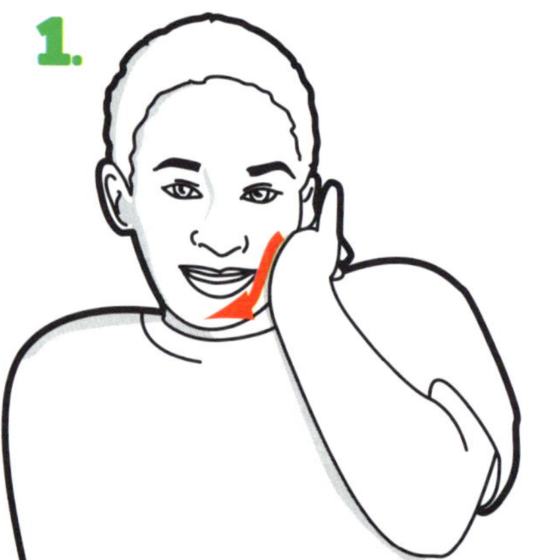

2.

Another word for sorry is "apologetic."

# Sorry

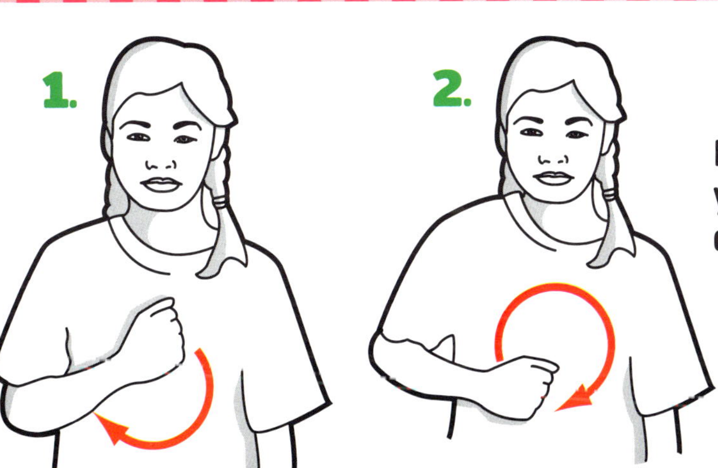


Place your fist on your chest. Circle around twice.

Another word for thoughtful is "reflective."

# Thoughtful

Make a loop around your temple area. Repeat.

Another word for thrilled is "elated."

# Thrilled

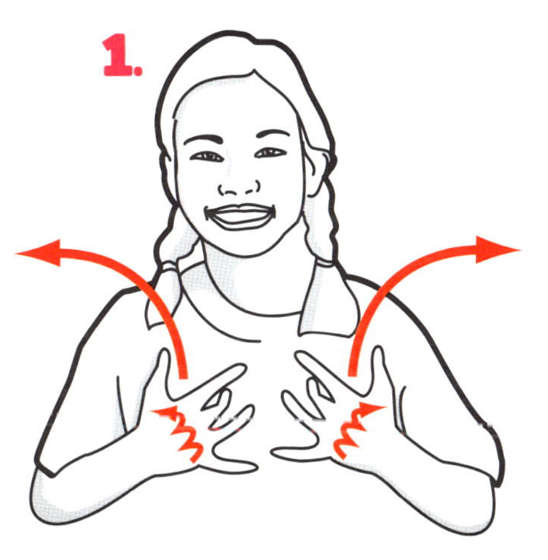

Wiggle your fingers on your chest, then bring them up and outward.

Another word for upset is "agitated."

# Upset

Make the "K" sign. Point downward. Then flop and point upward.

Another word for worried is "anxious."

# Worried

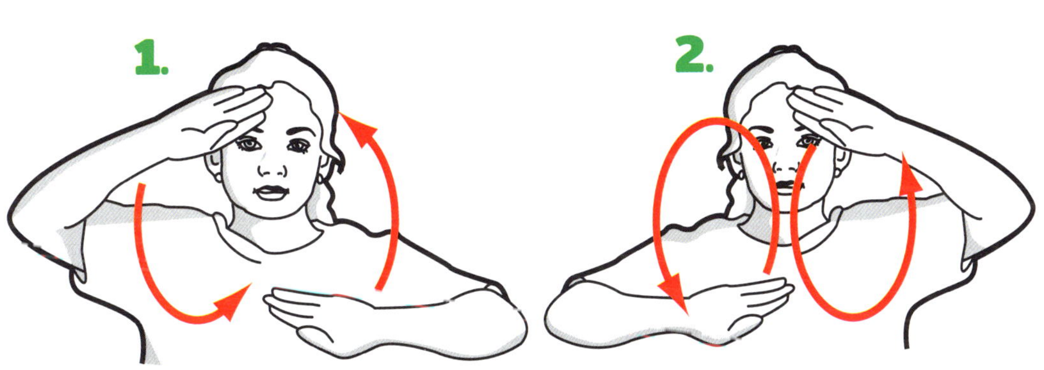


Using your flat hands, make small circles in opposite directions. Move as if you are swatting away worries that are troubling you.

## Wonder More

- How much did you know about American Sign Language (ASL) before reading this book? Do you already know some ASL signs? What new signs did you learn?

- Some words or specific names don't have signs. In these cases, you can spell the individual letters of the word, which is called fingerspelling. Look at the alphabet chart on page 23. Can you sign the letters in your name?

- With a partner, pick three signs from this book and practice them together. Are you able to understand each other? Is ASL easier or harder than you thought it would be?

- Think of a word about a feeling or emotion that isn't in this book. Try spelling out the word with fingerspelling. Then look up the ASL sign for the word. Where can you find more ASL signs?

# Sign Language Alphabet

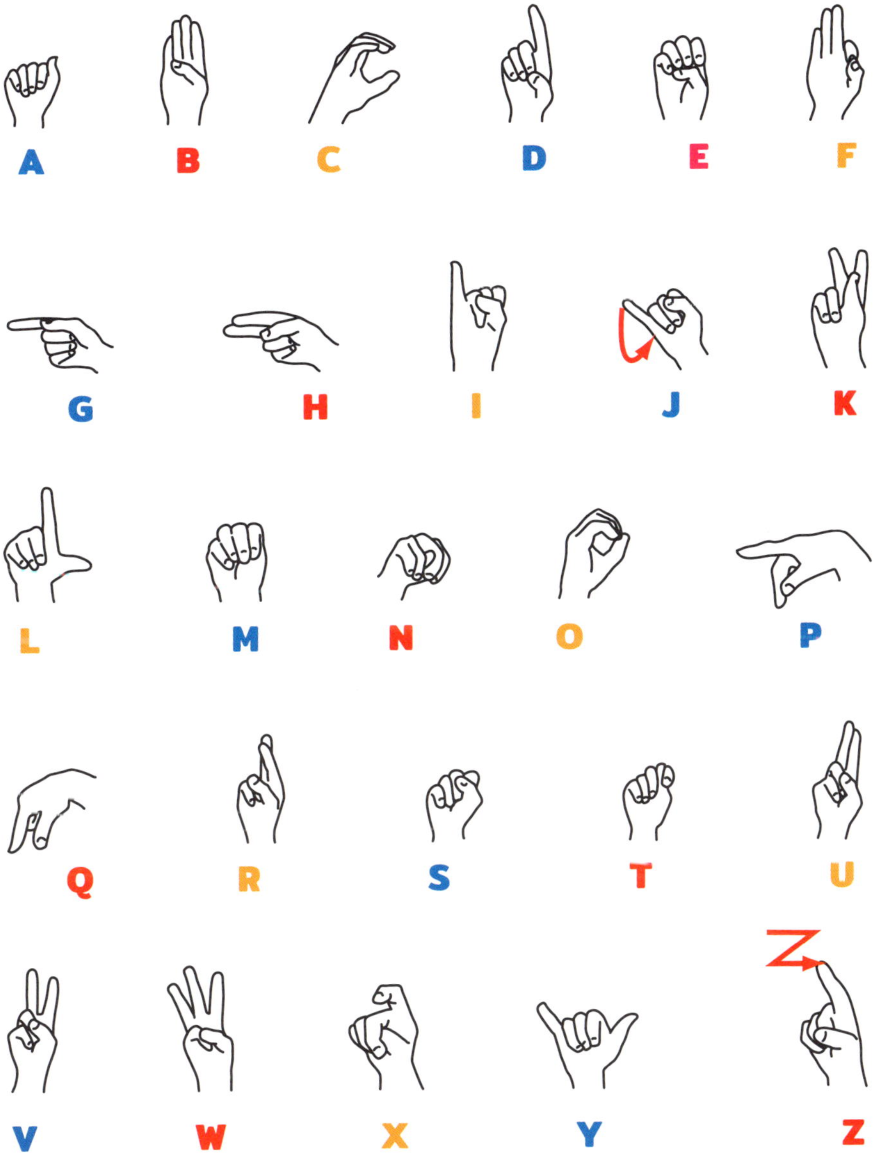

A B C D E F

G H I J K

L M N O P

Q R S T U

V W X Y Z

# Find Out More

## In the Library

Adams, Tara, and Natalia Sanabria (illustrator). *We Can Sign! An Essential Guide to American Sign Language for Kids*. Emeryville, CA: Rockridge Press, 2020.

Brakenhoff, Kelly, and Theresa Murray (illustrator). *Never Mind! (Duke the Deaf Dog ASL Series)*. Lincoln, NE: Emerald Prairie Press, 2019.

## On the Web

Visit our website for links about American Sign Language:

**childsworld.com/links**

*Note to Parents, Caregivers, Teachers, and Librarians: We routinely verify our web links to make sure they are safe and active sites. So encourage your readers to check them out!*

# A Special Thank-You!

Thank you to our models from the Program for Children Who are Deaf and Hard of Hearing at the Alexander Graham Bell School in Chicago, Illinois.

Aroosa is in third grade and loves reading, shopping, and playing with her sister, Aamna. Her favorite color is red.

Carla is in fourth grade. She enjoys art and all kinds of sports.

Deandre likes playing football and watching NFL games on television. He also looks forward to going to the movies with his family.

Destiny enjoys music and dancing. She especially likes learning new things and spends much of her time practicing her cursive handwriting.

Xiomara loves fashion, clothes, and jewelry. She also enjoys music and dancing. Her favorite animal is the cat.